Americans All biographies are inspiring life stories about people of all races, creeds, and nationalities who have uniquely contributed to the American way of life. Highlights from each person's story develop his contributions in his special field — whether they be in the arts, industry, human rights, education, science and medicine, or sports.

Specific abilities, character, and accomplishments are emphasized. Often despite great odds, these famous people have attained success in their fields through the good use of ability, determination, and hard work. These fast-moving stories of real people will show the way to better understanding of the ingredients necessary for personal success.

Jacqueline Cochran

FIRST LADY OF FLIGHT

by Marquita O. Fisher

illustrated by Victor Mays

GARRARD PUBLISHING COMPANY
CHAMPAIGN, ILLINOIS

To George R. Olsen, my dad

Library of Congress Cataloging in Publication Data

Fisher, Marquita O.
  Jacqueline Cochran.

  (Americans all)
  SUMMARY: A biography of the woman pilot who
organized and commanded the Women's Airforce Service
Pilots during World War II and became the first
civilian woman to receive the Distinguished Service
Medal.
  1. Cochran, Jacqueline—Juvenile literature.
[1. Cochran, Jacqueline. 2. Air pilots] I. Mays,
Victor, 1927–   illus. II. Title.
TL540.C63F57   629.13′092′4 [B] [92]   72–14368
ISBN 0–8116–4580–0

Picture credits:

Brown Brothers: p. 26
Jacqueline Cochran: pp. 75, 92
Culver Pictures, Inc.: p. 66
Wide World Photos: pp. 38, 78 (both), 89

International Standard Book Number: 8116–4580–0

Library of Congress Catalog Card Number: 72–14368

Contents

1. The Girl Who Didn't Belong

Jacqueline Cochran laughed and patted the elephant's trunk. "Good boy," she said as she poured another bucketful of water into the tub for the big animal to drink. Some of it ran out onto her bare feet. Her dress, made from cotton flour sacks, was wet and streaked with mud. But she didn't mind.

Jackie, a skinny child, was about six years old, but she was determined to show the circus people she could do a good job. Then when they moved on in the morning, perhaps they would take her with them.

How wonderful that would be, she thought. The circus people had been jolly and kind. No one had screamed at her and beat her as mama did at home. There was plenty of food here too. Why, there was even some bread left over after dinner—a sight Jackie had never seen before. Yes, to go with the circus would be wonderful!

Jackie wondered if mama, papa, or her two older brothers and two older sisters had missed her yet. No, she decided, remembering the night when she was lost in the woods and no one had cared enough to look for her.

The elephant's tub was filled now. All the people who had crowded the fairground earlier that evening had left for home. Most of the lamps were dark. Jackie curled up on a pile of straw near the elephant. She allowed herself only a moment to stare up at the summer sky filled with stars; then she closed her eyes. The circus would be leaving at dawn, and she wanted to get up early.

When morning came, Jackie awoke with a start and looked around. The fairground was empty. Jackie's brown eyes filled with tears. But she had learned long before that it did no good to cry. There was nothing to do now but go home.

In 1916 home for Jackie was a one-room shack in a poor mill town in northern Florida. It stood on wooden posts at the edge of a swamp. There were no window panes. Sometimes bats flew about in the attic, and bedbugs marched up and down the walls and floors. There was no electricity or running water. Jackie slept on the floor.

Jackie hated going back to the crowded

little house, but she had nowhere else to go. She didn't want to face again the scoldings, the disorder, and the constant hunger.

"Why can't we live better?" she asked mama a few days later.

"Where do you think we'd get the money?" mama shouted, angered by the question. "The lumber mill doesn't pay papa and the boys enough to buy food, let alone fix this place up."

But Jackie knew that other people who were just as poor seemed to manage better. She wished mama would try to be more clean and orderly!

As the summer wore on, Jackie did her best to help find things to eat. Sometimes she caught fish or crabs. Often she would wait by a dock until a fisherman felt sorry for her. Then he might give her a mullet

from his catch. Once she was so hungry that she stole a sweet potato from a farmer who was cooking a potful for his pigs.

Jackie often dreamed of escaping to far-away places where there would always be enough food, a warm bed, and shoes to wear when it was cold or raining.

Later that summer, when Jackie was sitting outside the house, mama's voice came through the window. "They left Jackie for us to bring up," she was saying to a visiting neighbor. "They made us promise we would never tell."

Jackie didn't wait to hear any more. She ran quickly away where no one could see her. Then she jumped up and down for joy.

"I'm glad I'm not one of them," she almost shouted.

Now she became even more determined to leave home. But until she could find a way, Jackie went back to school when it opened.

2. School Begins and Ends

Jackie had started the first grade the year before, but on the third day the teacher tried to whip her with a ruler. Jackie struck back, then ran for the door. She didn't go back that year. But now a new teacher from Ohio had come to the little schoolhouse. Jackie decided to try school once again.

Jackie liked the beautifully dressed Miss Bostwick at once. She was strict with the children and made them work hard. She slapped them on their hands with a ruler when they misbehaved. But she was fair.

Two days after school began, the teacher took Jackie aside. "I'll pay you ten cents a week if you'll bring firewood to my room at the boardinghouse every day. Will you do it?" Jackie could hardly believe her good luck.

Right after school that day, Jackie got some wood and managed to climb the steps to the second floor. Miss Bostwick was waiting for her in the doorway.

Jackie's brown eyes widened in delight as she peeked over the armload of wood. She had never seen such a cozy room. A little stove glowed in the corner. Pretty pictures decorated the walls. Flowered curtains hung at the window. Jackie wanted to return again and again.

Each day she took Miss Bostwick several loads of wood. Finally Miss Bostwick had to say, "Jackie, if you bring me any more firewood, I won't have room for my bed!"

Jackie and the teacher soon became good friends. After school, Jackie would go home with Miss Bostwick and sit spellbound while her teacher read books aloud by the hour. Jackie began to dream of the faraway places and interesting people Miss Bostwick read about.

During the next two years, Miss Bostwick spent many special hours with

Jackie. Besides teaching her to love books, she taught Jackie to take pride in her appearance. Now every morning Jackie filled a big tub with cold water from the pump and gave herself a good bath. Mama and her sisters laughed at her "foolish ways."

Miss Bostwick also gave Jackie a comb and ribbon and showed her how to fix her long, dark-blonde hair. She bought Jackie a new dress—the first ready-made dress she had ever owned. Jackie no longer felt ashamed of the way she looked in school or anywhere she went.

Although no one else in the family went to church, mama sent Jackie once a month when the priest came to town. Jackie wondered if it was because of a promise made to her real parents.

The priest, like Miss Bostwick, became

16

Jackie's friend. Both seemed to be telling her, "You can rise above all this. Study, work hard, find the stars." With their help, Jackie became happier and continued to learn each day.

But Jackie's happy times did not last long. At the close of her second year of school, Miss Bostwick told her gently, "I'm going to move back to Ohio."

Jackie's heart filled with sadness. For her no other teacher could ever take Miss Bostwick's place. She continued to study and read, but she never again went back to school.

3. Jackie Finds Work

That fall the wife of a mill worker asked, "Jackie, would you help me take care of the house and kids until our new baby comes? I'll pay you ten cents a day."

Jackie, who was now about eight years old, eagerly accepted the job. She did the housework and watched the children. She even cooked the meals, although she had to stand on a box to reach the stove.

Soon other people nearby heard that Jackie was a good worker. She was hired by one family after another. One time she even delivered a baby because there was no doctor or neighbor to help.

December came, and Jackie saw a beautiful doll in the window of the general store. She longed for it with all her heart.

"It's not for sale," the storekeeper told her. "Each time you spend 25 cents here, I'll put a slip of paper with your name on it in this bowl. The person whose name I draw on Christmas Eve wins the doll."

Jackie had earned four dollars, but no one had the money to pay her yet. So Jackie found other jobs to do. She drew

well water, scrubbed clothes, and worked until her hands bled. When she had saved 50 cents, she ran to the store.

"I want two chances on the doll," she said breathlessly. She bought 50 cents' worth of presents for her sisters and for Willy Mae, the two-year-old baby of the oldest sister. But the important thing to Jackie was that she had a chance to win.

Early Christmas Eve Jackie hurried to the store for the drawing. She was standing right beside the storekeeper when he pulled the slip of paper from the bowl. He paused, lowered his glasses and read, "Jacqueline." The doll was hers!

Jackie flew home with the prize clutched in her arms. She flung open the door and held the doll up for the family to see. Mama turned away from the stove and frowned. "You're too big for that," she

said. Papa grabbed the beautiful doll and gave it to Willy Mae. It was all Jackie could do to hold back the tears.

The Christmas season passed, and a few weeks later the sawmill closed down. It was time to move on. People were saying that the cotton mills in Columbus, Georgia, needed workers. So the family picked up what few belongings they could carry and walked three miles to the railroad station. They climbed into a caboose for a free ride on the next train to Georgia.

Finally they reached Columbus. What luck! The mills were humming day and night. Even eight-year-old Jackie got a job and was promised six cents an hour. She would work from six o'clock in the evening until six o'clock in the morning and would be off all day Sunday.

Jackie had never been happier!

4. Jackie Learns a Trade

Jackie's job at the mill was to deliver huge bobbins of thread to the weavers. All through the night she pushed a heavy cart from one noisy loom to another. Lint hung in the air like fog and made her cough. Her bare feet ached. There was no place to sit down, even during the half-hour lunch break. But Jackie was earning money, so she did not complain.

At the end of the first week of work, Jackie eagerly waited in line to collect her $4.50 paycheck. Pictures of all she might buy raced through her mind. But when she got home, mama took the money away from her. The next week, Jackie gave mama only three dollars and kept a dollar and a half for herself. Then she went to a street peddler.

"I want some shoes," she told him.

The peddler reached for some plain brown ones.

"Oh, no," she said and pointed to a pair of high-heeled shoes—the kind she had seen well-dressed women wear on the street. "I want those."

The peddler smiled. Her feet, like her hands, were large for a little girl. Still he had to search the cart for his smallest pair of high-heeled shoes. Jackie paid him, put on the shoes, and stumbled proudly away. They were the first shoes she had ever owned.

Before Jackie was ten, she was put in charge of about fifteen other children. She and her family worked very hard to buy enough to eat and to pay the rent. They suffered in the heat of summer when the mill was hot and stuffy. In the winter, chilly air seeped through the cracks in the walls, and the workers were cold.

While they worked, Jackie talked with the other girls.

"Someday I'm going to be rich," she told them. "I'm going to own a big car and pretty clothes and travel all over the world."

Her friends laughed at Jackie's dream. The world of comfort and excitement seemed too far away.

Finally the people at the mill decided to ask the mill owners to make working conditions better and to pay the workers more

When Jackie was a little girl, children were
hired to work the machinery in cotton mills.

money. When the mill owners refused to
do these things, the workers went on strike
and left their jobs. Jackie walked off with
the others.

Weeks passed, and still the mill owners
would not make any changes. The workers
still refused to go back to their jobs. They
had no money left for rent or food.

Then one day Jackie heard that a woman
named Mrs. Richler needed someone to

help her at home and in her beauty shops. Jackie went at once to the Richlers' house. A dark-haired woman answered the door.

"I'd like a job," Jackie said at once. She didn't want to give the woman a chance to say no, so she kept talking. "I can cook real good. I'll work hard. Look how big my hands are. I can learn real fast and . . ."

Mrs. Richler smiled at the spunky girl and said, "Anyone who can do so much at such an early age should be given a chance. Come in, my dear. I'd like you to meet my family."

Jackie stepped into the nicest house she had ever been in. Mrs. Richler introduced her to Mr. Richler and their six children. Jackie could tell at once they would be kind to her. When Mrs. Richler offered her $1.50 a week plus her room and meals, she quickly accepted.

Every weekday morning at five o'clock, Jackie got up to help with the breakfast and house cleaning. Then she went to one of the Richler beauty shops where she cleaned the floor and sinks and mixed bottles of shampoo and hair dyes. At night Jackie helped fix dinner and wash dishes.

A few months later the workers went back to the mill even though the company had made no changes. But Jackie stayed on with the Richlers.

Mrs. Richler followed the teachings of the Jewish religion faithfully. She taught Jackie what was right and what was wrong just as she taught her own daughters. Jackie soon felt like one of the family.

Jackie quickly learned the skills needed to become a beauty operator. By the time she was thirteen, she could operate the

permanent-wave machine, a new invention.
Now she was earning $35 a week.

She found out that mama and papa were
even worse off than before. Jackie was old
enough now to understand how hard it
was for mama to run a household with so
little money. Each week she gave mama
some of her pay. Jackie saved most of the
rest. By the time she was fourteen, she had
saved several hundred dollars.

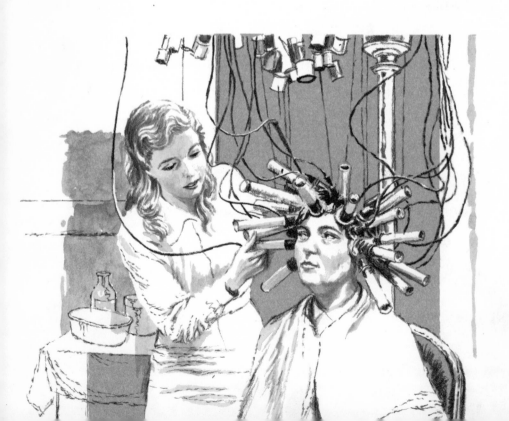

Then one morning, while Jackie was inside a booth waving a customer's hair, she overheard a salesman talking to Mrs. Richler.

"A shop in Montgomery would buy one of my permanent-wave machines if they could find an expert operator," he said. "Do you know of one?"

Jackie thought quickly. She could operate a permanent-wave machine as well as anyone, better than most. She pulled the curtain of the booth aside.

"I'm the expert you're looking for," she said.

Within a few days she had said a fond good-bye to the Richlers and her friends. She promised to keep sending money to her family.

Jackie was on her way to a new life in Montgomery, Alabama.

5. Out on Her Own

Jackie settled quickly into a cozy rented room and went to work in the department-store beauty shop. One of the customers, Mrs. Lerton, was a judge in the Juvenile Court. She liked Jackie and became almost like a mother to her. She taught her how to sew her own clothes and do needlework. She helped her to meet nice young people. Soon Jackie was going to lots of parties. She and her friends had fun driving around in the Model T Ford she bought with some of her savings.

One day Mrs. Lerton was watching Jackie's quick but gentle movements as she worked on a customer. "You are so clever with your hands, Jackie," she said, "and you do like to help other people. Did you ever think about becoming a nurse?"

For the next several weeks, Jackie thought about what Mrs. Lerton had said. Jackie had been working in the beauty shop for two years now. She liked the work there, but she decided that nursing would enable her to help more people. "Yes," Jackie decided, "I will become a nurse."

Mrs. Lerton helped her to make the arrangements, and soon Jackie moved into the hospital and began her studies. As always, Jackie worked hard and learned quickly. She took a real interest in all the patients. Even on her days off, she went into the wards to shave and cut hair for the people who were unable to help themselves.

When Jackie finished the three years of training, she moved to a small mill town in Florida, where she became the nurse for a poor, busy doctor.

One day Jackie and the doctor were called to a lumber camp for an emergency. They rode on a logging train about fifteen miles into the woods. As they walked toward the camp, they could hear a man moaning.

"His leg is crushed," a logger explained as he led them to the clearing where the man lay on the ground.

While the doctor examined the leg, Jackie asked the men to build a fire and heat a tubful of water. When the water was boiling, she put the doctor's instruments into it, including the saw they had

brought along. The man's leg would have to be cut off.

Jackie and the doctor worked quickly. When the operation was finished, there was nothing more the doctor could do. He went back home, but Jackie stayed at the camp to take care of the patient. At night she slept in a chair while a logger kept watch. Every four hours she would be awakened to change the patient's bandages. A few days later, when Jackie was sure he would live, she returned home.

Jackie had taken this job because she remembered her life in Florida, and she knew how much the poor people needed help. They had no money to pay for the food and housing they needed. They had never been taught the importance of being clean.

One night Jackie sat alone caring for a

sick woman. As the hours went by, she thought about her work. She began to see that she alone would never have the time, energy, or money to make a real difference in the lives of all those who needed help. By morning she decided that being a nurse no longer satisfied her.

"I will need money to help people," she told herself. "I have to go somewhere and find a way to earn it."

For the next two years, Jackie tried one job after another. She liked driving around the country selling various products. She liked working in beauty shops.

When Jackie was about 20, she took a job at Antoine's, an expensive beauty salon in New York City. During the winter months she worked at Antoine's salon in Florida. Her list of happy customers grew, and so did her bank account.

Jackie's new friend, Floyd Odlum. Their chance meeting would change the course of Jackie's life.

After work, life was exciting and fun for the pretty girl with the long, blonde hair. She loved parties and dancing, and won several ballroom dancing contests. During quiet times she became so skilled at needlework that one sample took a prize at a country fair.

One night at a dinner party in Florida, Jackie was seated next to a slender, handsome man. She didn't know he was a very rich businessman.

"I'm Floyd Odlum," he told her, smiling.

Jackie liked his quiet manner and warm sense of humor. She hoped she would see him again. He seemed to like her too.

As they talked, she told Floyd, "I'd like to work for a cosmetic company that has stores selling beauty aids across the country. It would be fun to travel from store to store and help to build business."

"You would need wings to do all that!" He laughed.

Wings! The idea of flying caught her imagination. She began to picture herself in the cockpit of a plane, flying from one business meeting to another.

But Jackie was still in Florida, and she had to be at work early the next morning. She left the party before midnight, knowing that both flying and Floyd Odlum would become important in her life.

6. Jackie Gets Her Wings

On the first morning of her three-week vacation, Jackie went to an airfield near New York City for her first flying lesson. "Husky," the pilot, showed her how to control the movements of the airplane with the stick and rudder pedals. He explained how the throttle controls the power of the engine. Jackie was eager to learn, so she listened carefully.

It was time for takeoff. Jackie held her breath. The plane roared down the runway and lifted. Jackie's heart began to pound with excitement. She knew then that she was going to become an aviator.

When they landed again, Husky explained what she had to do before she could get a pilot's license. "It usually takes two or three months to learn everything for the test," he added.

Jackie gasped. "I have only three weeks."

The big pilot laughed. "You'll never do it!" he said.

But Jackie spent every moment she could learning to fly. Only two days after the first flight, Jackie landed the old Fleet trainer, and Husky climbed out. "It's all yours," he said, closing the door behind him.

Jackie, alone in the plane, shivered with delight. She pushed the throttle in and headed down the hard dirt runway. In a few moments the wheels left the ground,

and Jackie was on her first solo flight. The roar of the engine was one of the loveliest sounds she had ever heard. She felt as light as the fluffy cloud floating nearby.

Then suddenly the engine stopped. The only sound was the whooshing of the wind as the plane moved through the still air like a paper glider. The plane slowed down. If it did not stay at a certain speed, Jackie knew it would stop gliding and go into a deadly spin. Her hands tightened on the stick. "Don't panic," she told herself. "Think!" She remembered what she had learned and pushed the stick forward. The nose dropped down. The plane picked up speed.

Jackie looked down and nervously searched for the field. Hooray! The airstrip was close enough to glide down to.

She sighed with relief. Then she directed the powerless plane toward the runway. Her first solo flight ended with what pilots call a dead-stick landing!

Floyd Odlum was now back in New York City. When Jackie told him what had happened, he laughed. "If you did that well on your first solo, you can surely earn a license in three weeks."

The men at the field, too, began rooting for her. They liked the way the pretty 22-year-old girl examined the engine and didn't make a fuss when she got grease on her hands. They admired the way her bright, dark eyes studied the charts and heavy textbooks. They were amazed that she could look at a page and later see it in her mind almost like a picture.

Before the three weeks were up, Jackie was able to tell Floyd, "I did it! I have my private pilot's license." How happy he was for her!

In 1932 there were few women pilots, and Jackie was determined to be a good one. But this would take time. Jackie thought over the idea of starting her own cosmetic business. "Then I can plan my day so I can spend more time flying," she said. She was glad she had saved enough money to do this.

During the next two years, Jackie was very busy. She flew all over the country getting her new business under way.

At the same time she became a more skilled pilot. She learned to find directions by the positions of the stars. At that time, airplane radios carried messages only in the dots and dashes of Morse code. She mastered that too. Jackie learned how different kinds of airplane engines worked and how they could be repaired. She practiced flying blind, using the plane's instruments to find her way in bad weather. She became the first woman to make a completely blind landing.

By 1934 Jackie was a skilled pilot, and her business was doing well. She was ready for a new challenge; so she decided to enter her first air race. A friend, Wesley Smith, agreed to be her copilot.

Most of the planes flown in air races were loaned to pilots by the manufacturers. Thus new equipment could be tested. The manufacturers hoped that their planes would win, because more people would then choose their models.

The prize money was $50,000, and Jackie hoped to claim part of it. But she wasn't thinking of herself alone. There were others to care for.

46

Papa had died, but mama and others in the family still depended on her support. Willy Mae was now grown with a little daughter of her own. Jackie paid for them to go where Willy Mae could find a better job. In return for that help, Jackie told Willy Mae that she wanted back the doll she had won that Christmas Eve so many years before. "I don't believe anyone should get something for nothing," Jackie said.

The race Jackie and Wesley entered was to begin in London, England, and end in Melbourne, Australia. The little Gee Bee plane they planned to fly was not quite finished. They took it to England by ship, and mechanics worked on it all the way across the ocean.

Two days before the race, Jackie and Wesley climbed into the plane to fly it for the first time. One of the seats had not been put in yet, so Jackie had to sit on a big wooden cracker box. As soon as the two pilots took off, they could tell the plane was not as safe to fly as they could have wished.

When they came in for a landing, the plane hit the ground so hard that Jackie thought they'd broken a wing!

But when they checked the plane for damage, they found none. They learned that the plane always landed like that!

At dawn on the morning of the race, the planes from many different countries were lined up on the runway. Jackie and Wesley taxied the Gee Bee into position. They would be the seventh plane to take off.

Jackie looked out through the canopy at the thousands of people who had waited through the night to watch. "They seem almost as excited as I am," she thought.

Now it was time for the Gee Bee to take off. The crowd strained to watch as it raced down the runway. They could tell the pilots were having some trouble getting off the ground. The engine didn't seem to have enough power, but the plane rose at last, cleared the field safely, and climbed into the bright sunrise.

Jackie and Wesley breathed easier. They began to think that they might reach the first refueling stop in Bucharest, Rumania, ahead of the others.

7. Flying Firsts

From the start, the two pilots worried about the troublesome engine. Then, while flying over the snowcapped Carpathian Mountains in eastern Europe, they saw that the needle on the gas gauge for one tank pointed to empty. Jackie pulled a switch so that the engine would get its fuel from the full tank. But the engine sputtered and stopped. Wesley Smith opened his canopy and got ready to jump. He waited for Jackie. She reached for her canopy. It was stuck. "I can't get out of the plane!" she gasped.

The plane glided closer and closer to the mountaintops. Jackie twisted one fuel-line switch, then the other. Suddenly the roar of the engine sounded again. The pilots exchanged happy smiles. Then Jackie saw what had happened. She wrote a note and handed it to Wesley, since she could not make herself heard over the engine noise. The note said, "When the switch says ON, it means OFF. When it says OFF, it means ON."

But that was not the end of their troubles. As they came in for the landing at Bucharest, one wing flap became stuck. The other moved only a little. The plane was thrown out of balance. They climbed, went around the field, and tried again to land. The flaps stuck again. Jackie struggled to loosen her canopy and finally succeeded. They made signs to each other:

"We'll have to jump if we don't make it this time."

At last they managed to get both flaps in up position. The plane touched down on the runway fast.

Jackie and Wesley knew the plane was not safe enough to continue in the race. They were bitterly disappointed.

When Jackie talked it over with Floyd later, he told her he hoped she would continue racing. The following year, she decided to enter one of the biggest and most important races in the United States —the Bendix Transcontinental Air Race. The pilots were to start in Los Angeles, California, and finish in Cleveland, Ohio.

The winner would receive a prize of several thousand dollars. But to Jackie, as to most pilots, racing was more than a chance to win fame and fortune. It was an opportunity to contribute more information about the science of flight.

When Jackie tried to sign up for the race, she was told, "Sorry, this race is not for women." Jackie would not accept that. She went to each man who was to fly in the Bendix and asked him to sign a paper which said he did not object to her racing. Only after every man agreed was she permitted to enter.

A few days before the race, Jackie noticed that the engine of the plane she was going to fly no longer ran smoothly and evenly. A man from the company that had provided the plane asked her to withdraw from the race. She refused. She could not back out now.

On the night of the takeoff from Los Angeles, fog rolled in so that the end of the runway could not be seen. The plane

ahead of Jackie's roared down the runway. Suddenly there was a crash, and the
plane burst into flames. The pilot, who
was a friend of Jackie's, was killed.
Jackie sat in her plane feeling sick with
shock and sorrow. Photographers gathered
around to snap her picture. They asked if
she was still going to fly.

A man from the company that owned
her plane ran onto the field. "Call off the
flight," he begged her again.

Jackie left the plane to telephone Floyd.
"What should I do?" she asked when she
finally got through to him.

They talked about the choices she could
make. But he left the decision to her.

Jackie was not afraid of dying. She had a strong belief that a person's spirit lives on after death. She was certain that death came only when it was time to die, and not before. Yet she wondered if her strong desire to enter the race was making her overlook its real dangers. After considering the possibilities carefully, she decided to stay in the race.

Jackie would use her instruments to make a blind takeoff into the wall of fog. A fire truck and an ambulance stood by. As she started down the runway, the engine of her plane did not put out the power she expected. But trying to stop would have meant crashing into the fence at the end of the runway. So with a prayer in her heart, Jackie pushed the engine to its limit. She caught her breath as she felt the wheels leave the ground.

But Jackie's plane was so low her radio antenna caught on the fence, and it was pulled off. She had no radio, but she was airborne. The engine shook. It overheated. Still Jackie flew eastward.

At dawn, she could see the Grand Canyon ahead. But she could also see what pilots feared most—an electrical storm. As she approached the storm, Jackie had to make an important decision. Should she risk flying her overheated plane through the strong winds, rain, and lightning or should she turn back? She wanted to continue. Good sense told her to go back. Full of disappointment she turned the plane and headed for the near-est airport.

The race was lost, but Jackie knew that she had won something—the Bendix would never again be closed to women.

8. A Bride Becomes a Winner

A few months later, on a lovely day in May of 1936, Jacqueline Cochran said, "I do," to Floyd B. Odlum. Jackie glowed with happiness.

"Floyd is at the center of everything Jackie does," a friend remarked, "and she is interested in everything he does."

Floyd encouraged Jackie to continue flying. Encouragement was what she needed. Several times she had nearly lost her life in flying accidents. She again entered the Bendix Race in 1937 and was disappointed when she came in third.

60

"It's the number on your plane," many people warned her. Jackie looked at the number 13 and laughed. Superstitions were a part of her. She felt certain that number 13 would someday bring her good luck.

Then, in 1938, she entered the Bendix Race for the third time.

It was about three o'clock in the morning when she climbed into the crowded cockpit of a little Seversky pursuit plane. She checked the oxygen tube and the radio. A soda bottle, half-filled with water, was propped nearby. It held a glass tube so she could sip the water without taking off her oxygen mask. She kept a few lollipops handy, too, to help keep her mouth moist.

Her maps, or charts, had been marked many weeks earlier when she first began to plan and train for the flight. Now she attached them to a string, then tied one end of the string to her leg. If the charts should get tossed off her lap during "bumpy" weather, she would be able to pull them back.

Trouble rode with her in this race too. She ran into bad weather. The gas tank in the right wing became blocked. The fuel would flow only when she tipped the plane.

But when the wheels of her plane touched the ground in Cleveland the next afternoon, she knew she had won first place. Two hundred thousand people stood and cheered.

A judge rushed to the runway to lead her to the winner's platform. He found her combing her hair and fixing her makeup.

"Where is my husband?" was her first question. She pushed through the cheering crowd. In a few minutes, she and Floyd were together. She clutched his arm. "I'm not afraid to fly across country," she said, "but in a crowd like this, I'm afraid without you!"

With each passing year, Jackie's life became more like her little-girl dreams come true. Jackie's cosmetic company did well, and Floyd's work continued to be successful. Among their friends were kings and presidents.

The girl who had once lived in a shack was now the owner of a new airplane and the mistress of three homes. Her favorite house was on a 600-acre date farm in the California desert. She and Floyd spent most of their time there.

But Jackie didn't forget what it was

like to be poor. Neither did Floyd. The son of a small-town minister, he had also known difficult times during his childhood and had worked to pay his way through college. So Floyd nodded encouragement when Jackie told him she wanted to help the needy. Sometimes in her travels when she saw a child who was poor and un-cared for, she checked into the family life and made arrangements at once for help. She also saw to it that dozens of children had the chance to go to school.

When Jackie wasn't with Floyd or man-aging her business, she was flying. She entered many more races, testing many new products. She tried out new engines, fuels, instruments, and propellers. She tested helmets, masks, and spark plugs. Some of these failed to work, and several times Jackie was nearly killed. But each

Jackie's picture was taken in front of her plane after a record-breaking flight between two California cities in 1939.

test provided information, so the product could be made safer.

"What has been the greatest satisfaction you've had from flying?" Jackie was often asked.

"The testing I've done and the information developed from it," she would answer.

During this exciting time in her life, Hitler came to power in Germany and was trying to take over much of the world.

Other countries in Europe had risen against him, and World War II was raging. Jackie often said to Floyd, "I wish I could do something to help in the war effort." Floyd was already busy helping the president improve the economy.

One day at a luncheon in Washington, D.C., Jackie talked with the chief of the Army Air Corps, General H. H. "Hap" Arnold. He told her about the men who were flying American planes from Canada to England for the use of the British air force. Then to her surprise General Arnold said, "Why don't you fly one of the bombers over to England? We need every plane we can get over there, and besides that, your flying would call attention to the need."

It was the kind of job Jackie had been hoping to find.

9. Jackie Goes to England

Jackie could not have guessed that most of the American pilots would be opposed to a woman flying bombers to Great Britain. One man took equipment out of the cockpit to keep her from being tested for the first flight. Others threatened to go on strike if she flew the plane. But finally they reached an agreement. Jackie would be listed as first officer and fly the plane. Captain Carlisle, a navigator who was also a fine pilot, would take the plane off the ground and land it.

At last everything was ready. Captain Carlisle took off at dusk, then turned the controls over to Jackie. Captain Carlisle went to his table and stayed there charting their position. The radio operator sat in his tiny room behind the pilot's cabin. Jackie handled the big plane easily, following every rule in the book which she had studied carefully.

After a few hours, Jackie looked out in delight. There were the northern lights! But clouds hid the ocean from view as the plane raced on through the night. She and the crew ate sandwiches and hard-boiled eggs and drank tomato juice.

Then, just before daybreak, tracer bullets shot up around them through the darkness.

Captain Carlisle rushed forward. "Maybe they spotted us on radar," he said.

"Maybe it's one of our ships, and they think we're an enemy plane," Jackie suggested.

The radio operator came running out of his room with his signal pistol. He opened the hatch and fired a flare that glowed the color that was the signal for the day. They hoped the bullets were coming from a friendly ship that would understand the

signal and stop firing. But none of them really thought that the ship would be able to see the flare through the cloud cover below.

Jackie flew straight ahead, getting out of the danger area as quickly as possible. They checked the plane and were happy to find there was no damage.

Soon after daybreak, Jackie caught sight of the coast of Ireland and began to follow a difficult air route. First she directed the plane one way, then the other, as written in her orders. The route was changed each day to make it impossible for enemy planes or submarines to figure out which way the Allied planes would fly.

Twelve hours after takeoff, they arrived in Scotland. It had been a night Jackie would never forget.

Reporters rushed up to the pretty American flier after the bomber landed. "How about some pictures, Jackie?" they begged.

Jackie shook her head. "These slacks need pressing. I can't be photographed in them."

The reporters laughed and waited until Jackie changed into a pretty dress. Then she posed for pictures. Writers everywhere called her "the glamour girl of aviation."

After a short stay in England, Jackie returned to the United States.

The next morning at nine o'clock, she received the message that President Roosevelt wished her to be at Hyde Park for lunch that day.

"You're joking," Jackie said, but soon she realized it was no joke. A police escort rushed her by car to the president's home.

After lunch, she and the president went into his office. "Tell me what's going on in England—through a pilot's eyes," he asked her.

She told him about all she had seen and heard. They talked for nearly two hours.

Several days later, she was called into General Arnold's office.

"An English official has asked me if you would organize a group of American women pilots and take them to England," he told her.

Jackie had seen for herself how much England needed experienced pilots. Still, she hesitated.

"We'll be in this war someday too," she said at last. "I'm certain of that. Then all our pilots will be needed here."

"Yes, but the time has not yet come for that," General Arnold answered. "In the meantime, I hope you will accept the job in England. Learn what you can from the experience. Someday we'll need you to organize women pilots here."

Jackie talked with Floyd before deciding to take the job. They agreed that winning the war came before anything else. Both would work toward that end. Their life together would have to wait until the world was once again at peace.

Jackie began flying all over the country searching for experienced women pilots who were willing to fly for England. Twenty-five were finally chosen and trained. They were sent to England, with Jackie in charge as flight captain.

Jackie, like the rest of the women, mastered the dangerous task of flying planes

Jackie flew planes in wartime England as a flight captain in the British Air Transport Auxiliary.

in wartime England. The women flew planes from factories to airports and from one airport to another. They transported people and equipment. Each job they did freed a British pilot for combat work.

Soon after the United States entered the war, a brief message came from General "Hap" Arnold. "Come home," it said. Jackie went back to Washington as quickly as possible.

10. Women's Air Force
Service Pilots

General Arnold asked Jackie to begin at once to find women pilots and to organize a training program for them. She chose Houston, Texas, as the base where the women would be trained. Letters from women fliers began to flow in. Jackie flew from city to city to interview each pilot personally. At last she chose 25 that she felt would set a fine example for other women pilots. They met at the field in Houston.

Jackie looked over the different kinds of old training planes collected for their use. She knew it would be useless to try to get better ones, for there was a war-time shortage.

Jackie took charge of the training program, and after several months of hard work, the first class of 25 was ready to graduate. But several days before graduation, Jackie became very sick. The doctor ordered her to stay in bed at the Cochran-Odlum Ranch in California. But Jackie was determined to go to Houston to take part in the graduation.

"It's 200 miles from here to the Phoenix Airport," her doctor reminded her. "You can't sit up that long in a car."

Jackie thought and thought. Finally she had an idea. She picked up the telephone and called the local undertaker.

"I would like to hire a hearse to drive me to Phoenix," she told him.

Jackie pins the wings of a military pilot on a newly graduated WASP. Below, members of the new unit take part in practice maneuvers.

A few hours later, the long black car pulled up at the Phoenix Airport. Jackie climbed out of the back and boarded the plane for Houston.

It was a shining moment for Jackie when she handed each member of that first graduation class a diploma.

As soon as Jackie grew well again, she returned to her post as director of the WASP—the Women's Air Force Service Pilots.

Jackie's scars from a much earlier operation were giving her a great deal of trouble and pain. Sometimes she was barely able to stand up. An air force doctor showed her how to stop the pain for a short time, but he also gave her a list of hospitals.

"Never be any farther than four hours' flying time from any of these hospitals," he warned her. "You might need emergency treatment at any moment."

Yet Jackie kept busy day and night running the program. She even helped design the uniform the girls wore—a bright blue suit with army air force wings pinned to the jacket. While flying, they wore fur-lined overalls and boots, and a parachute.

It was not long before dozens of small groups of women fliers were working at different fields where Jackie had set up programs. During the first week of work at a field in North Carolina, two planes crashed, killing two women pilots. Saddened and shocked, Jackie flew at once to the field. The other women pilots were afraid. Some found excuses not to fly.

"The planes aren't safe," they told her.

Jackie took every plane up for a long,

hard test ride. Each had at least one thing wrong with it.

"But what plane in wartime hasn't something wrong?" she asked the pilots. "These are as safe to fly as any."

The women returned to their work, but a few days later another plane crashed. The pilot was rushed to the hospital with a skull fracture.

Jackie was determined to find the cause for the crashes. Finally the report came through—sugar was found in the gasoline, and sugar in gasoline would stop the engine in a very short time. An enemy agent had been at work!

Doing what she could to win the war was Jackie's main concern. When she heard from the White House that many of the products she had tested were now being used by the air force, she glowed with pleasure. But there was no time to sit back and smile over past accomplishments. Directing the WASPs kept her busy day and night.

Before the war ended in 1945, more than 1,800 women had entered the training course. More than 1,000 of them graduated and flew with the air forces.

At the end of the war, Jackie received the Distinguished Service Medal for her special part in the war effort.

11. Breaking the Sound Barrier

In the years following the war, Jackie traveled all over the world, often with Floyd. She managed their homes well and made certain that food and money were not wasted. She spent many hours reorganizing her cosmetic business. She had had no time to oversee it during the war, and it was losing money. She also developed a new interest in politics, but flying was still first among the things she liked to do. She continued to test planes and enter races.

Jackie had only to look up at the growing number of jet trails tracking the sky to see that jets would be the aircraft of the future. "I'm not going to be left out of that part of aviation," she promised herself.

Because of her experience in high-speed flying, Jackie became a flight consultant, or adviser, in 1952 for a Canadian company that built the Sabre Jet F-86. Part of Jackie's job was to make speed tests at Edwards Air Force Base in California, where the weather was good and a speed course for timing already set up. The company hoped that with the plane's new engine, she would break a woman's record or two which would result in more business for the Canadian company. Jackie agreed, although she was only interested in breaking men's records.

Jackie went into strict training for the test flights. She went to bed early each night so that she would be well rested. She controlled her diet and exercised so that her body would be strong and healthy.

Jackie worked hard. She studied each part of the engine. "What does this valve do?" she asked one mechanic. "What does such high speed do to the fuel lines?" she asked another flier.

Colonel Charles "Chuck" Yeager was the first person to fly faster than the speed of sound and live to tell about it. He helped her in every way he could.

During Jackie's third flight in the Canadian Sabre Jet, Chuck Yeager flew in a jet nearby as an observer. Only he knew what she planned to do that day.

Jackie flew her jet plane higher and

higher. As she rose, the sky around her became a darker blue. The sun was like a burning ball, but there was no sunlight as we know it here on earth. There, on the edge of space, she looked up and saw the stars. It was still midday.

Jackie kept the plane flying upward until it reached 45,000 feet, nearly 9 miles above the earth. Then, after moving the plane into the proper position, she pointed the nose of the Sabre Jet straight toward the ground and began her full power dive. She hoped to pass safely through the speed zone where dangerous shock waves build up. She was going to fly faster than the speed of sound! Many experienced pilots had tried to do this and had failed. She hoped to be the first woman to succeed.

She checked the reading on the Mach

meter, an instrument that measures such high speeds.

"Mach .97," she said into the microphone so that Chuck could hear her. She was nearing Mach 1, the speed of sound.

"Mach .98."

The left wing suddenly dipped. Then the plane tilted wildly the other way and the right wing dipped. Then the nose began to act as if it wanted to turn the plane on its back.

"Mach .99," Jackie said quickly but with confidence.

The plane shook as the air began to build up like a wall in front of it. Jackie acted quickly to control its movements.

"Mach 1," she called out.

"Mach 1.01." She was through the dangerous sound, or sonic, barrier!

Inside the plane there was silence. At

Jackie brings in her F-86 Sabre Jet for a landing at Edwards Air Force Base.

that speed, Jackie was flying so fast she was leaving the roar of the jet engine behind her.

She began now to pull gently out of the dive. Again the plane jerked wildly as she slowed it to below the speed of sound.

When Jackie landed and got out of the plane, friends at the air base rushed to congratulate her.

"I was so happy I felt like I was walking ten feet off the ground," she later told Floyd.

Before the plane was returned to Canada, Jackie set three world speed records and dived three times past the sonic barrier.

Messages poured in from people all over the world. Among them was a special letter of congratulations from her good friend President Eisenhower.

Later Jackie received the International Flying Organization's gold medal "for the outstanding accomplishment by any pilot, man or woman, during 1953."

In the years that followed, Jackie was often in poor health, but she continued to fly. Many more awards came her way, including the Legion of Merit and the Distinguished Flying Cross.

Helping other people, especially children, continued to take up much of her time. Her husband, too, seemed never too busy to reach out and help another person even though he was too sick to lead a very active life. In all of their years together, Jackie had learned that he was one of the kindest, gentlest, and most generous human beings she had ever known.

In 1953 Jackie was voted Business Woman of the Year. She enjoyed her business success, but it no longer seemed important to her. She sold her Jacqueline Cochran line of cosmetics several years later.

In 1954 Jackie wrote a book about herself. "What I have done, others can do also," she told her readers. The title of the book was *The Stars at Noon*.

Seeing the stars at noon while teetering on the edge of space was only one of the many thrills that flying brought to her life. She once flew around the Taj Mahal in India by moonlight and circled around the crater Vesuvius in Italy. One time she saw a huge bow around the moon, like a rainbow—only it was night, and the bow was a silver color.

Jackie climbs out of the cockpit of the F104G Starfighter. She had truly become "the first lady of flight."

She was the first woman to land a jet on an aircraft carrier; the first woman to fly to Mach 2, twice the speed of sound; the first woman to pilot a jet across the Atlantic.

In 1963 her tests of the military fighter plane, the F104G Starfighter, helped to clear up its reputation as a plane that was dangerous to fly.

Jackie's name and list of accomplishments now hangs in the Aviation Hall of Fame in Dayton, Ohio, along with those of other leaders in aviation.

At a banquet in 1971, Jackie was admitted to the Society of Experimental Test Pilots. When the society's president introduced her to the hundreds of test pilots present, he told them, "Jacqueline Cochran has done more for aviation than many of you men."

Loud applause burst through the hall.

It was a proud moment for Jackie. Even though she was no longer test flying, her heart and mind went out to those who still braved the dangers of the sky for the good of aviation.

"With my last breath," she said, "I'll be on the aerial sidelines cheering those who are carrying on."

Index